Life lessons from the gam

THE GOLF BALL DOESN'T LIE

Joe : Carla
you can't play a
Birdie Game
with a Bogey attitude

Larry D Hood

Larry Hood

emerge
publishing

www.Emerge.pub

THE GOLF BALL DOESN'T LIE: Life lessons from the game of Golf

Copyright ©2023 Larry Hood

Published by:
Emerge Publishing, LLC
9521 B Riverside Parkway, Suite 243
Tulsa, OK 74137
www.emerge.pub

Library of Congress Cataloging-in-Publication Data:

ISBN: 978-1-954966-28-4 Paperback
E-book available exclusively on Kindle

BISAC:
SPO016000   SPORTS & RECREATION / Golf
SPO012000   SPORTS & RECREATION / Essays

Printed in the United States

CONTENTS

The Golfer's 23rd Psalm

The Lord is my caddie,

I shall not slice.

He makes me drive down green fairways,

He leads me over quiet water hazards,

He restores my short game.

He guides me in the ways of etiquette

For His name's sake.

Even though I shank it into

The valley of the shadow of out of out-of-bounds,

I will fear no penalty, for You are with me.

Your putter and driver, they comfort me.

You prepare a table for me in the presence of other duffers.

You anoint my putter with oil,

And the cup is too big to miss.

Surely, birdies and pars will follow me all the days of my life,

And I will dwell in the clubhouse of the Lord... Forever.

From the Holy Bible, 23rd Psalm

Foreword by Stephen Belk

I met Larry Hood in my freshman year during the late summer of 1982 at Angelo State University. I'd say he's my best friend but looking back he was more of a big brother and a spiritual mentor during those early years. Over 40 years of friendship, Larry has been a spiritual brother to not only me but so many others I cannot venture to guess. Larry and I attended college together, lived together, played a lot of golf together, achieved our dreams and held each other thru the deepest sorrows of life. Larry's gift has always been his ability to minister to people through his word and now through his writings. He has had a great passion for life and people, and it has been the breath of life amongst those in need and really seeking God.

While this book is about golf, it teaches us of life for those who love the game. Furthermore, reading this book may provide insight into a wonderful game for those who know little about golf. As I read this book, I was reminded of Larry gift of words and metaphors. I hope you enjoy this book as much as I did. Finally, I think this book is best presented in recalling a memory of playing golf with Larry. One day during one of life's lows, Larry and I played golf near the DFW airport. We always played golf to get away, enjoy life together and share the game we loved. The golf course at DFW provided not only high rough, sand traps and water but loud highway traffic and airplanes flying directly overhead. On one par four, Larry's tee shot landed in a low ravine over 150 yards from the green. I walked past him towards the green to see my ball by the green and as I turned around, I could not see Larry, nor could he see me or the green. I yelled for him to hit his shot, so he would know I was out of harm's way. I could hear the strike of the club but couldn't see the ball, that is, until it landed on the green and rolled into the hole for an eagle two. I was speechless, with no expression on my face as if I expected nothing less from my best friend. As he approached the green, laughter and passion poured out of him, and life's sorrows were gone.

Stephen Belk PsyD

FOREWORD BY KEVIN RIGGS

I too have a love for the game of golf and for the space that it holds in my life. At every level of ability, golf is the game played knowing that you will never master it, you can only play it to your best effort and mindset on any given day. Like life, golf is what a golfer must do, but not necessarily with routine success and not even guaranteed enjoyment! The game is full of emotions from high to low, from satisfaction to disgust, but for most golfers, and what Larry clearly shares in TGBDL, what we most value golf for is the relationships and shared lives with those with whom we play.

Larry's passion for golf is real but is no comparison to his passion for people. Larry has a gift for counseling and encouraging those around him while not letting pity or defeatism rule the day. He makes space in life to help others see the sometimes obvious, and sometimes not so obvious evaluations that we have to travel through to succeed, adjust, persevere, and perhaps occasionally simply survive. I am honored to have Larry as a great friend and brother in the Lord and appreciate his ability to see that the comparisons of our attitudes about golf and about living can be of great benefit in our journey.

Kevin Riggs

THE GOLF BALL DOESN'T LIE

Golf is an amazing game; I've been golfing since I was about 14 years old. One day, I was invited by a friend to join him and his dad at the local public course. Man, it was really early and a little chilly for a spring day. I remember the sights, sounds, and smells of this new world; the dew on the freshly mowed grass, the aroma of the flowers and trees, and the sounds of birds and trees rustling in the breeze. I don't remember how I played that day (all bad, I'm sure), but I do remember the feeling of being in a special place, something that touched me deep down, and it is still there every time I step onto a tee box.

I'm at the point in my life where I've "made the turn" I'm on the "back nine" of my journey. There is a flood of memories and experiences whenever I play. I "remember" is a part of my thoughts, heart, and soul.

I remember...
- *My first summer playing golf with my friends.*
- *The feeling of teeing off at sunrise; the sights, sounds, and smells.*
- *Looking down a long fairway as the sun sets in the evening.*
- *My longest drive.*
- *My longest putt.*
- *My first birdie.*
- *My first eagle.*
- *The first time I broke 100.*
- *The first time I broke 90 at my favorite course (it took me 30 years).*
- *The first time I broke 80.*
- *Moments with my best friend from college.*
- *The first time Linda (my wife) and I went to our favorite golf retreat.*
- *The first time my wife, Linda, beat me.*

"Remembering" is an important part of who I am, for there was also real life going on. There were things going on in my life that were challenging and, at times, overwhelming but being able to go to those memories reminds me that there still is life, joy, encouragement, and hope in the midst of the hard. I live and play with the knowledge and expectation to make new memories, not just live off the old ones.

Over the years, I've come to see the truths and lessons of life in the game of golf. When I struggle, lose my way, fail, and become disappointed in where I am in life,

I "remember" the moments when things were good, when I was good. Like golf, life is a series of moments, opportunities, and experiences. One bad shot, one bad hole, one bad game doesn't have to define me and my life. How I play my way out of those moments does. My attitude, perspective, and response will determine how I face my next challenge.

You can show up with the best, cockiest attitude, dress up like a pro, have the best equipment, and talk smack but when you step up to that first tee and give it your best shot, that, along with all your following shots, tells us all we need to know about your game; you see... **the golf ball doesn't lie.**

WHY I LOVE GOLF

I fell in love with golf mainly because I was with my friends. We weren't very good, but we sure had fun. We laughed, made fun of each other's bad shots, and cheered when someone accidentally made a good shot. Then we started playing with the older guys, and some of them were good! Every now and then, they would take the time to give us a tip or two, encouraging us when we did well or making fun of us for a bad shot. As time went on, I got the hang of it; I learned the rules, the proper stance and grip, and how to get out of trouble. I started having moments where I made more good shots and scored better, and I started enjoying the game over just having fun. Now I wasn't just playing for the fun of it; I was able to compete, not just with those in my group but also with myself. The challenge to be better. I've played with those who just don't get it; they don't see the enjoyment in the game of golf. It is a study of frustration for them. So, many have not pursued the game. I see the same in our relationship and faith in God.

First, they have never had a friend who has really shown them the game. Oh, we've all been invited to go to church, but that's about it. Humor me as I tell a little story:

Imagine that a man is invited to go to a "Golfer's Church"; the pastor is a retired, successful pro golfer. Every Sunday, he gets up and tells stories about golf; he also teaches the fundamentals of golf in Sunday school. This man becomes enthralled and passionate about his church. He goes to all the classes and all the services. He gets to the point where he is asked to teach one of the classes. This is all fine and good, but I see just one problem. HE HAS NEVER PLAYED THE GAME AND EXPERIENCED IT FOR HIMSELF. He is living off of someone else's experience of the game.

This is just my observation, but if all you do is watch, you might have an appreciation and respect for "the game," but it won't be real until you actually play and experience for yourself the joys and heartaches; you will never have nor understand the passion of those who have.

Second, they have never been around those who "get it," those who know God, have done it a long time, and are pretty good at it. These "pros" don't just know the rules but have a passion and enjoy the "game" and the challenge to see how good they can be.

I fell in love with golf because I was around good golfers who loved golf. It was their passion and a part of their soul. I fell in love with God much the same way. I've been around some amazing people who have a heart and passion for God. They didn't just know the rules and teach them to me, they showed me what it meant, how they got there, and the difference it could make in their life, my life, and others.

Third, it's personal. They have a point of view, an opinion, and a perspective that comes from their own experiences and moments with God. In the course of their life, they have made it through the hard by believing and holding on to what they know from being there before. Like golf, life is more about changing your swing (attitude) rather than getting new equipment or giving up the game. Over the years, I have taken those lessons and what I have learned from observing and made the game my own. Life and getting older have molded my style, form, and approach to golf and life. In spite of my aches, pains, and limitations, I have figured out my game. When I golf with someone for the first time, and they see my stance, swing, and approach to the game, after a few holes, they say, "bud, I don't know how you hit it straight, but you do, I wouldn't know how to begin to help you. " There are fundamental truths and principles to golf and life that can't be avoided or changed to be successful, but each one of us has our own unique rhythm and approach. We just have to discover them.

WHAT MOTIVATES ME

I got to thinking (yes, it hurt… a lot) about what it is about golf that means so much to me. I admit I enjoy getting better and seeing my handicap go down, going out, and competing with my friends. I'm not good enough, nor have a strong desire to play in tournaments, maybe someday. What I enjoy about golf is sharing it with my friends with the possibility of something amazing happening; a great drive, a miraculous shot out of the rough, an approach shot close to the cup, or even that seeing-eye putt from a mile out.

I realized that in writing this that I have lived my life pretty much the same. Take, for instance, my love for Horseshoe Bay golf resort, as it is not only because it is an excellent venue to play, but it has a lot of memories for me. I came to find this golf haven way back when I was in my twenties. I was married and living in Fort Worth, Texas, and was planning on going to Longview for my best friend's wedding.

On the Wednesday before the wedding, I received a call from my buddy:

Steve: "What are you doing this weekend?"
Me: "Um, going to a wedding. "
Steve: "Nawwwww, you want to go on the honeymoon?"

It seems that his bride-to-be had changed her mind about their nuptials. That weekend I met my friend in Horseshoe Bay, Texas, for a three-day "honeymoon," where we golfed and had an amazing time. We have been going back ever since; it has become another part of the bond of friendship and brotherhood that I share with Steve. Over the years, it has been the touchstone and time of respite as we have faced the difficulties and joys of our lives. For just a few days, we can step out of our "normal" lives and reconnect to a time, place, and bond that was, and is, a special part of our lives. All built around the game of golf, for a few days, we can get together and reminisce about old times, good and bad, compete, encourage, and create new memories.

One of my favorite memories is when I was able to golf with Steve's two boys when they were about 8 (Austin) and 10 (Josh). I had his youngest as my partner, and on one of the most challenging holes, a par three, 140 yards, and a hit over the water, this little man lined it up and put it on the green, an amazing shot! He then stepped up to his putt and holed it out from about 40 feet… BIRDIE! I was so proud of this young man. So glad I could be a part of this moment. I believe that one of the blessings of life is being there when something amazing happens, whether it be in my life or another.

Another favorite memory at Horseshoe Bay is when I took Linda for the first time. We had not been dating long, and I wanted to take her to my favorite place. I knew she golfed but wasn't sure if she was as passionate as I was. I had planned on us golfing for two days and then doing "her thing" on the third day. After our second round of golf, I told her how much I enjoyed and appreciated us getting to golf, but we would spend the last day doing what she enjoyed. Her response was, "Can't we golf?" I knew then we were soul mates, and I was right. Golf is still an important part of our relationship.

In fact, when we were planning our vacation in 2017, I let her pick the place. I found her looking up Myrtle Beach, S. C. , and golf courses we could play. We spent a week playing on some of the best and most beautiful courses that I've ever played on. We created a lot of new memories and met some wonderful people everywhere we went.

I said all this to say; golf has been the constant in my life and many of my relationships. It has given me a place and reason to focus on what is good about my life, to see the beauty around me, the gift of people that I love, and that none of us have to "play the game" alone.

THE COURSE

The average course is usually around 7 miles long and takes about 3 1/2 to 4 hours to play a round. That's a long way and a long time. The course is designed to provide a challenge for all golfing abilities. Each course is designed with the idea of rewarding good shots and punishing bad ones. There's a reason it's called "the rough," the "fairway," and the "trap. " Think about it, the course is "predestined" for all the golfers, it doesn't change, and the par is the same for every player, usually 72. Even though the course is the same for everyone, it is not "pre-determined," that's up to each golfer and the quality, skill, and fortune of each shot. Yes, you can make a good shot with bad results or have a bad shot with good results, that's golf, and that's life. I don't know if you've ever been there, but I have known times when I felt that life was just out to get me. I did the best I could, played by the rules, and it still turned out bad. I know the heartache, frustration, and disappointment. I admit, I've entertained the idea of going back to old ways and habits, even though I knew that it wouldn't fix anything but probably add to my misery.

At that moment, I had a choice, I could let my emotions guide me, or I could trust my "game. " I know it's not much comfort, especially when you're in the middle of your frustration and know it's not going to get better for a while, if ever, and finding the courage or "want to" to hang on and see it through. It's easy to quit, go back to old habits and find momentary comfort in your misery. But if you want your "game" to get better, you have to trust your "swing," hang in there and "play through. " The challenge is not to settle, make excuses, lose your dream, or give up on what could be… what you could be.

> *"A positive attitude may not solve all your problems, but it will bother enough people to make it worth the effort. "*
>
> *- Anonymous*

I was watching the USGA Open in Shinnecock Hills in 2018. Now the Open is known for being a tough challenge, and this year was no exception. Brooks Koepka outlasted the rest of the field with a one OVER par score. Compare that to Dustin Johnson's nineteen UNDER par at the St. Jude's Classic or Patrick Reed's fifteen UNDER par at the Masters. Yes, the course was tough, intentionally so, and there was drama. On the third day, the course was almost unplayable. Wind, greens that dried out, and challenging pin placements made it almost impossible to score well. Therein lies the lesson…

Golf, as well as life, brings out our best or worst. Where most players and commentators complained and reacted in less than glowing terms, they definitely showed their character and attitudes. Then there were those who recognized it for what it was, a challenge to be overcome. Yes, it wasn't fair. Some had an advantage by playing earlier when the greens were more receptive. Yes, the rough was, well, rough. The winner was one who endured and overcame, first, with his attitude, then with his resolve.

We all spend our lives trying to negotiate "the course," those that find themselves on a course that plays to their strengths and gifts are blessed. It almost seems too easy, not that anything is without a challenge. You still have to compete to win. It's when we have to "play the course" that it gets tough. You just can't "come out of your shoes" on every drive; the rough is tough, the traps are the size of Texas, and the greens are mean to you. You have to think, believe in your game, have patience, and have an attitude that gives you a chance to compete, even win. And if that doesn't work… relax, enjoy the moment as much as you can; it can't get any worse and play for another day.

32

PLAYING FOR... SECOND?

Back in the day (yep, I'm old), the best golfers were Jack, Arnie, Lee, Gary, Tom, Greg, and a few others. They had skill and were usually at the top of the leaderboard on the final round on Sunday. It wasn't until Tiger came along that he changed the game. He didn't just show up to compete; his whole mindset and preparation were to destroy the competition. The other golfers were, well, golfers. They looked like golfers, lived golfer's lives, and did golfer stuff; Tiger, however, was an athlete. He had been groomed and prepared since he was a little child to be an athlete who golfed. It was an amazing thing to watch him take over a tournament and run away with it. I remember one golfer, who was being interviewed, commented, "Yeah when Tiger is 'on,' we realize that the rest of us are playing for second place. "

The difference? One man saw the POSSIBILITIES of winning the tournament, knew he was CAPABLE of winning, went out, and played EXPECTING to win; therefore, he knew it was PROBABLE. The others looked at the competition and came to the limited conclusion that "it's NOT possible for me to win because he's so good," "I'm

NOT capable enough to win," and "there's NO WAY I can expect to win," so I'm probably NOT going to win. " Do you see the difference? One man looks within and sees the opportunities, while another sees the obstacles. In golf and life, I listen and counsel people all the time who sit and tell me why they aren't, can't, and never will be successful. You know what? They're right. What I listen for is what I emphasized earlier; What is possible? What do you think you're capable of doing? What do you expect to happen? Then I can, with fairly good confidence, tell you what is probably going to happen.

I was golfing with a young friend the other day, and as we stepped up to the first tee, he said, "I just want you to know I'm not very good. " You know, he was right. I get it; not all of us can be "pros" at everything but have some dignity. I've had people come up to me before they spoke at a service or conference and ask what advice I would give them. I simply tell them, "don't tell us that you're not a good speaker; we'll find out soon enough. " I realize when I step up to that first tee, "I'm even par right now!" My goal is to keep it going. In whatever I'm doing, confident or not, I realize that every challenge is a chance for glory, to rise above my own expectations and do something memorable, even amazing, to see the opportunity and not the obstacle, to draw strength from within, rather than let my fears come from without.

Now we have a new generation of athletes who play golf with a whole new attitude. What was once considered a gentleman's game has been taken over by warriors. There is an intensity and energy that fuels competition and has brought out the best in the older golfers as well as the next generation. I think it's time that some of us do the same in our own lives.

THE CLUBS IN YOUR BAG

The USGA allows a golfer to have 14 clubs in his bag. The standard set of clubs has 12 clubs, which means the individual golfer can add 2 extra clubs as he deems appropriate. I don't know about you, but I've become pretty comfortable with the clubs in my bag. Over the years, I have come to know which club I can hit for a given distance and situation.

When choosing your club, you have to understand your ultimate goal and purpose… get the ball in the hole. Duh, right? You would think so. At the tee box, on a long hole, your goal is power and get it down the fairway. Stay away from the traps and the rough; give yourself the best chance for an eagle, birdie, or par. The second or third shot takes a little more finesse and accuracy, depending on your skill and how well you know and trust your club selection; the goal is to get it on the green or close. Finding the rough or the trap means you're going to have to be creative; you better know and trust your game. When you get on the green, it is about reading the green and touch. Sizing up the situation, being able to read the green and bring it home.

We all carry a "bag" in our everyday life. I love my golf bag; Linda bought it for me when we were on vacation. It has a "Margaritaville" theme about it. It makes a statement about how I want to be seen as a golfer and person. That I have a little bit of an attitude, a sense of humor, and fun. The bag you carry says a lot about you, your brand of clubs or golf balls, and your favorite sports team. I've even seen clubs in a duffle bag… rebel! We are subtly, or not so much, telling the world, "THIS is how I define myself, WHAT I identify myself with, WHAT I am proud and passionate about. " It says something about us. No matter what your "bag" is, it still is just a carrier for what really counts, your clubs. To me, our clubs represent our faith, what you turn to when situations in life get challenging. It is the emotion, attitude, or action that is your "go-to club. "

I asked a friend, who is a pretty good golfer, what club he would use from 135 yards out. Without hesitation, he said, "8 iron". No question, no thought; he knew what club he was going to use and had confidence that it would get the job done. That is your "faith. " As I said, I'm not talking about your "religion" or your "beliefs. " I'm talking about what you trust; what's your "go-to" when you need it to count? It is what you trust to get the job done. Your "faith" shows in your attitude and confidence… or not. One of the most courageous things anyone can do is to realize his "club of choice" doesn't accomplish his intended goals. I know some men who have only ONE club in their "bag," their driver. They come to most, if not every situation trying to power their way through life. It's called anger. What kind of score would you have if the ONLY club you used was the driver? Every shot you took, you put all your power into it. How effective would that be? Not very; if you don't understand or remember your goal, get the ball into the cup.

All of the clubs in our "bag" serve a purpose and have a place, but when we lose sight of our goal, we can allow our emotions and frustrations to determine our club of choice and how well we use them. Yes, there is a time and place for power, but as we get closer to our goal, it takes more purpose, skill, touch, and finesse to reach our goal. So, I guess the question is… What is your goal? Maybe you're not thinking about the "goal," maybe you're trying to punish the ball (life and those in it), only you know. If you have only one club that you trust to get the job done, are you ok with that? Are you ok with those you're "playing the game" with, for them to fear and be afraid of you when you pull that club out? Are you ok with knowing that you are affecting their game, not just for the moment but maybe for the rest of their life? It's not just the anger "club" that some men (and women) use; I know some that only use their putter. They believe that the way to handle the "course" is just to be passive and not make waves in life. It's good in a scramble, but that means you are putting all the responsibility on your partner to get through the tough part of the course. Are you ok with sitting back and making your partner do most of the work, emotionally, spiritually, and financially? Whatever "club" we use, it takes balance, skill, confidence, and purpose.

THE SWING

Whether it's off the tee, in the fairway, rough, sand trap, or green, whatever club you use, there is a constant… your swing.

> *"I got so caught up admiring my swing that I forgot to play golf. "*
> *- Howard Varley*

DEFINITION OF A GOLF SWING

"The golf swing is important to every golfer's game. To hit a golf ball, the golfer swings a club while standing at the side of a motionless ball positioned on the ground. Such a swing involves angular motion. In physics, angular motion is defined as the movement of a body about a fixed point or axis. " (Encyclopedia. com)

However you define it, your swing becomes obvious the moment you hit the ball. It's a skill, oh sure, there are those guys for whom it comes naturally. They have the build, natural rhythm, and tempo; it is second nature to them (god, I hate those guys). For others, they had to work at it; they practiced, took lessons, and earned their handicap (I'm jealous of those guys). Then there are those who go out and just give it their best shot. No gifts, no talent, no warm-up, just get out there and see what happens (I am that guy).

I've known guys who would go out and have a bad game, break clubs, blame the ball or weather, and then show up the next time we played with new clubs, balls, and/or a new bag. They can never get to that point that maybe it's something a little more "organic" and closer to home, like their "swing. "

In life, we all have a "swing" that is revealed in our **Attitudes, Actions**, and **Words**. No matter how you dress it up, it's OBVIOUS! We can't hide behind our intentions and excuses. So, stop blaming your "bad game" on everything and everybody else. Ok, we all know that guy who "just has it," yes, we hate him, but I bet you have some gifts of your own that you don't know about; find them. Next, figure it out… take a lesson, practice, read a book, and find someone who can teach you not just the game but the perspective, attitude, and spirit that makes a great golfer. Stop "wishing and hoping. " Figure your swing out!

I hear you… "Thanks for the advice, Mr. Wizard, but how do I SPECIFICALLY figure out my swing? It's obvious that I'm doing it wrong; how do I get it right?" I'm glad you asked. I've talked to those who know the game of golf, are better at it, and understand it more than I ever will, and here is what I've gleaned from their wisdom and experience.

"You can't play a birdie game with a bogey attitude"
- Larry Hood

If you want to go from "duffer" to "good" to "great"…

PRACTICE WITH PURPOSE

I'll be honest; I don't really practice; I hit balls. It is probably more of a warm-up than a session. Also, for some reason, a good practice session seldom translates to a good game for me. Pro golfers and outstanding golfers will tell you NOT to spend your time hitting your driver on the practice range BUT on your mid-irons and short irons. Yes, it's not as glamorous being good from the fairway; we LOVE being the "Big Dog" off the tee but remember your purpose… par or better.

Isn't that like life? I can talk a good game, be impressive in my delivery, and tear it up on paper or in my mind, but when I really have to perform, I choke. The difference? The pressure to perform. I experience this almost every time I speak, lead a conference, or counsel. I'm an animal in my preparation, practice, and mind, but when it's "showtime," it just doesn't come out as polished or as I hoped it would.

Don't get me wrong, practice is essential, even necessary, if you want to improve, but it is only a part of what it takes to be good or great. Prepare, practice, and perform with purpose.

STAY IN THE PRESENT

"The most important shot in golf is the next one. "
                                                    - Ben Hogan

I believe the hardest thing in golf is not letting a bad shot influence the next one. Whether it be a bad drive, iron shot, chip, or putt, it can ruin your mood and grove. If you let it get to you, it can change your attitude, therefore, your game. A wise man once said, "The ONE thing that I DO, I forget those things that are behind me, AND I FOCUS on the goal before me. " Notice that he said, "The ONE thing…". Wait! Doesn't the conjunction "and" connect the two thoughts? Well, yes and no, but we're talking about what we need to DO, and that is… FOCUS on the goal. You may be a better and stronger person than I am, but I don't have the ability just to forget, especially something that negatively affects me. However, if I can focus on the goal and what I am trying to achieve, then that "bad shot" doesn't have to translate into a "bad game." When I find myself in the rough or sand trap, I can see this moment as an obstacle or an opportunity.

The world's best golfers are not great because they keep it in the fairway, hit it close to the hole, or hole it out every time. They are great because they see the opportunity in every shot, even the bad ones. I looked up online the best shots of Bubba Watson, Phil Mickelson, and Tiger Woods. ALL of the awe-inspiring shots captured for posterity came AFTER horrible shots that left them in challenging, if not impossible, positions. So many times, in golf as well as in life, great things happen after some of our worst moments, IF we will just stay in the present.

CONTINUALLY WORK ON
THE FUNDAMENTALS

I know I talk a lot about the importance of a good attitude, but that is just one part of the whole. Another important aspect of golf, as well as life, is the fundamentals.

Fundamental (adjective): "Serving as or being an essential part of a foundation or basis. " (dictionary. com)

I was going to give you some wise, sage advice on the fundamentals of golf, but, like life, you have to figure it out for yourself and how it fits your game. In my research, I found a mountain of books and articles on the basics of the game. If you watch the Golf Channel, you'll see programs, commercials, and gimmicks on improving your game. There is a difference between understanding the basic principles and "doing it the same way someone else does. " Don't get me wrong; you're not going to have to reinvent the game of golf to fit you, but you are going to have to take the basic principles and make them your own. Every golfer has something that makes them unique, as well as every person. Where I believe we fall short is when we mistake fundamentals for style. Now don't get me wrong, I do believe it is important to have those we admire and emulate, especially in the stages of learning and discovery. I am grateful and appreciative of all the advice from those who are more talented, accomplished golfers than I am and probably ever will be in my life.

My friend Howard is a little older than I am and is about a three handicap. He has an easy swing and a low-key attitude to the game of golf. "Just take it nice and easy, pardner," is his motto. My buddy Billy, on the other hand, is going to "come out of his shoes" and try to hurt the ball. I've found that I need a little tension in my attitude and swing but still be friends with the ball. In spite of their different approaches to the game, they have found a way to make it work for them, and I'm trying to do the same. When I go out to the practice range, I am continually trying to find the rhythm and tempo that brings out my best, but if I don't have a good understanding of the fundamentals of the game, then I'm just hitting a ball into a pasture.

I hope you can make the jump to live in the same way. In our world today, we have those who are trying to "sell" us on their programs, commercials, and gimmicks. "If you just act like we act, talk like we talk, and believe what we do, then you'll be successful. " I'm not entirely distancing myself from this, but I want to live a life that is mine. I will listen, watch, and learn, but as I discover for myself the principles of life, I will make them my own.

54

PLAY WITH VISUALIZATION AND FEEL

I believe that this is what separates the average golfer from the accomplished one. Most of us "duffers" are just trying to make good contact with the ball and go "north and south," we're just trying to hit the ball in the direction of the hole. We spend our time wishing and hoping, depending on luck, fortune, or fate. Every shot is made with a little bit of fear, doubt, and anticipation. What I hear from folks in life is similar, "I think," "I feel," " I hope," but if you want to get better, you have to get to the "I know" part of life.

Good golfers have moved beyond the mechanics of the game and are able to see and feel every shot… they know. All the good golfers that I have been around and those I talked to all said the same thing; it starts on the practice range, getting to know your swing and knowing your clubs. They just don't "hit balls" but go out with purpose and a plan. The best golfers work on shots and situations, so when the moment comes on the course, they can see the shot and know the tempo and speed it takes to get to the hole.

In short, we need to do more than just know THE game; we need to know OUR game. When I'm with good golfers, I notice that there is something that separates me from them, it's confidence. It shows in their stance, demeanor, and swing, even when they make a lousy shot or are in a difficult situation. They have taken the time, practiced with purpose, and know their swing and clubs. You won't hear the terms; "if only," "I think," "I feel," or "I hope," the better golfers "know. "

BE CONSISTENT

Golf, as well as life, is about getting ourselves into a position to be successful. So, what do you do when things aren't going the way you want or need? A bad shot, a poor game, or even going into a slump is a part of the game and life. Every golfer has, or will, go through this. Whether you get through your rough stretch depends on where you put your trust.

Top golfers have inner confidence and know where to put their trust and where to turn to get back into the game. Every good golfer has developed a routine to get them in the right state of mind and preparation to make a shot. Almost every move is scripted and on purpose.

Trust is more than just mechanics; it involves our minds and emotions. It takes a lot of courage not to let circumstances be what defines how we respond to a given situation. We've talked about how our game is molded and shaped on the practice range, but it is proven on the course. The routines that we build into our lives allow us to succeed and excel. It's a great feeling knowing you can put your trust in yourself and have confidence no matter what "the course" brings.

60

KNOW THE POWER OF
ACCEPTANCE AND MOVING ON

Golf is a game where you better have a very short memory…

I might be wrong, but golf is designed to challenge our abilities and creativity. As hard as we try, there will come a time when we find ourselves in a situation that demands us to dig deep and make a shot that we have never dreamed of, much less anticipated or practiced. The ability to accept the outcome of every shot, good or bad, and move on to the next one sounds simple but is not easy. Part of our problem is we seem to attach our personal worth to our game. The ability to move on is being able to do our best in the present, minimize the damage, and let the past be the past with our sense of self intact. Golf is not just one shot or one hole. So many times, we allow the failures, disappointments, and defeats to carry on to our next shot.

> *"Three bad shots and one good shot equals par."*
> *- Walter Hagans*

A WORD FROM OUR PRO

"Golf is a game that can't be won, only played. "
- Bagger Vance

I had the opportunity to sit down with Bruce Sims, who is the golf pro at Ridgeview Ranch in Plano, Texas. I wanted to get a perspective from somebody who has made golf their life and work and maybe find out the secret to having a great golf game.

Bruce has been in the golf world for 41 years; he didn't grow up golfing but came into it in his twenties. He said that he immediately fell in love with the game and, in his first tournament, shot a 67 (I hate him). We spent about an hour talking about what motivates him still today, what he has learned, and what it takes to be a great golfer or, at least, a better golfer. Following are his thoughts…

"Golf is a one-shot game; you have to take every shot on its own merit and opportunity. What you think, how you approach every shot, and deal with challenge, frustration, and disappointment will determine the success of the next shot. We need to remember and be motivated by realizing that, even though we are out there with other people, we are playing against the course and ourselves first and foremost. To get better, we need to focus not on what's 'out there' but on what is within ourselves. Golf is a process that is played out with so many factors, the course, the weather, our set-up, our stance, our rhythm for that day, our mental state, and confidence. If all we focus on is the result, then we are going to struggle. "

There are no secrets about getting better at golf. The difference between a hack and a good golfer is the work, commitment, and desire one is willing to dedicate to the game. "A game" is a term that Bruce often used; "You can't buy a game," he said, "it's a game with a round ball and a stick with a head on it, go out and ENJOY it!" To get better, be honest with yourself, take your "if's," "if only," and "what if's," and do something about it! Through effort and purpose, turn those statements into "I did" and "I can do it. " Don't settle, and don't think it is going to happen by magic.

My final question to Bruce was, "What will you remember when you play your very last hole and look back on your life of playing golf?" His answer was, " I'll remember how much fun I had getting here... I hope I make par. "

COMPETE

Golf (noun): *"A game played on a large open-air course, in which a small hard ball is struck with a club into a series of small holes in the ground, the object being to use the fewest possible strokes to complete the course. "*

By nature, golf is a competition between yourself, the course, and/or others. It is a test of your skill, luck, perseverance, and endurance. Now, I bet at one time or the other, you've said, "I'm not concerned about my score; I'm just having fun. " Be honest; if you were shooting under par, par, or even close, would you still say that? Nice try, Pinocchio! We play because we love to compete; it is in our DNA to overcome and conquer all our obstacles, even ourselves.

Don't get me wrong, I still play for fun, but I always strive to improve. The proof of that? I keep score on every round. I'm usually (mostly) pleased every time I play. No matter what I score, I am there to compete, to get better. There is something inside me that challenges me to be better, not settle for mediocrity, to not accept any excuse.

I've never been the kind of guy who was just torn up IF I lost, IF I did my best, IF I competed.

There are many things I admire about pro golfers, but it is their attitude in any given situation that they can do something amazing, something special on any given shot. You can feel the energy, excitement, and expectation before the shot.

Has anybody done anything significant where they didn't have to overcome great obstacles, struggles, defeat, embarrassment, or even failure?

70

NOTICE

I have one word for you to focus on today... notice. Golf is a game that is usually played in the prettiest place in that city. It receives more attention and care than anywhere else. Whether it's a public course or a private one, it is a showpiece. So, notice... take a moment and be aware of your surroundings, the beauty (hopefully), the relationship you have with those you're golfing with, and the challenge of the game at hand. I've golfed with those who were so caught up with "the game" that they missed the life around them. Don't we all do that? Get so caught up in "winning," "success," and "playing our best" that we just don't notice what's going on around us.

I've had rounds that weren't going so well (ok, it was just bad, all bad); I'm frustrated, discouraged, and disappointed... I'm not having fun! Then there is Linda... Linda notices life on the golf course. I'm not so sure that she doesn't go golfing just to feed the "critters." On our home course, the little ground squirrels seem to know when she is on the course and come up to her for a snack, even taking it out of her hand... she notices. It reflects her heart and what's really important to her. Don't get me wrong;

she's there to compete and gets frustrated just the same, but she never passes up the opportunity to feed the animals.

I want to grow up and be like Linda. Amid the challenge and competition, she hasn't lost sight of the big picture… "life. " In some of the most challenging moments that I have gone through, she has helped me refocus and realize that "I'm going to be ok, we're going to be ok. In spite of this moment or place in our life, we have what it takes to get through this. "

In those moments, I stop, take a deep breath, and realize that there is more to this game than doing well, shooting par, or even winning.

BAD WEATHER

"There is no such thing as bad weather for golfing, only inappropriate clothing. "
— *Anonymous*

It was the last Sunday of 2017, about 40 degrees, drizzly and getting colder. Our "normal" routine was to spend Sunday afternoon on the golf course. Now my two golf buddies, my wife, and Howard, are "fair weather" golfers, or so I thought. I was sure that we would spend this afternoon on the couch in front of the fire, but as we got closer to tee time, I received a text from Howard:

> *Howard: "We playing?"*
> *Me: "Ummmmm, no. "*
> *Howard: "Why not?"*
> *Me: "Let me ask Linda. "*
> *Linda: "We're not playing?"*
> *Me: "Ok, this is getting weird. "*

Howard: "It's our last chance to golf this year."

So off we go. We geared up in our warmest clothes and still be able to swing a club, we looked like we were more prepared to snow ski than golf, but we were game. Our best game? Not even close. Fun? The best. Lots of laughter and friendship. We were on the 18th tee; it was now 34 degrees and drizzling; we all agreed that this was one to remember.

Sometimes it's just about the moment and making a memory. We get so caught up in the game that we forget that there is more to it than the score and hitting a good shot. Life is going to give us "bad weather," cold, rainy, and if you live in west Texas, 40 mph winds. There are a lot of good reasons to stay in, be safe, and wait for better weather, but what fun is that? Get up, get out there, and play for what it's worth. Make a memory, have a story, and give people something to question your sanity about.

OH, IT'S ON

Most of the time, when Linda (my wife) and I play golf, it's competitive, semi-cordial, and "almost" supportive, but on this one round, she told me on the first tee, "I'm going to whup (we say "whup" in west Texas) your behind today. Oh, it's on. " It changed the whole attitude of the round. Every good shot was praised, and every lousy shot was laughed at and highlighted. There's nothing like a little competition, friendly or not, to get your blood flowing. I love that part of the challenge that brings out our pride and drive to be better than our opponent, wife, friend, or not.

Without a doubt, one of my proudest moments of golf was the day that Linda beat me. No excuses; she had to play in the same wind I did. She won fair and square. Every part of her game was on, and I couldn't be more proud, but secretly, I'm going to do everything I can to make sure it doesn't happen again.

Maybe that's the issue I have with our world today. We have lost that "oh, it's on" attitude. We've replaced a spirit of competition with the spirit of "play nice. " I'm not advocating being a bully or arrogant but creating an opportunity for us to be challenged, to have something to lose, and also something to gain. I'm sure you've been in a place where the odds were against you, you knew you couldn't win, but you had to play anyway. At that moment, you had a choice; you could fold, give in, and play nice, or you could get in there, compete and see what happens. I hope you know that feeling where your desire to compete and overcome is greater than your doubts and fears… "oh, it's on!"

DAYS YOU JUST DON'T HAVE IT

I had been playing well in previous rounds and was feeling good about my game. I knew on the first hole that it just wasn't right. There was a feeling, almost a taste, in my mouth that wasn't right. Golf is about rhythm and tempo, something in your body that is just right or wrong. It either lines up or doesn't; well, on this day, it didn't. Shots that I usually have confidence in and hit well, putts that typically go in or are close, not only off but ugly. Now, this is not the first time that I didn't start off well; I'm confident enough in my game and know the course well enough to know that I can catch up and make things right… ummmmm, not this day. Bad, all bad. It started with disappointment, then discouragement set in, and finally, frustration. We finished 9 holes and talked about playing the back 9 or not.

There was still something in me that HAD to try; I couldn't just give up. You have to understand that Linda and I have a very "spirited" relationship when we're playing golf. We enjoy making fun of each other when we mess up, getting into each other's head (do you breathe in or out before you hit the ball?), and all-around giving each other… you know. It's all in fun, but it also raises our game, but on this day, she felt sorry for me. I HATED that! When we got to the pity part of my game, I was done. The last straw was on the 13th tee; I hit my driver, I thought pretty well, but it slowly, I mean, slowly rose into the sky, then dropped like a rock. Thank God I made it past the ladies' tee box! It was at that moment I thought, "Time of death…. I'm done. I just don't have it today".

FINDING YOUR SWING

This is a follow-up to my last chapter; I went golfing with a friend about a week after the disaster, that "inspired " my last thoughts. I went out early one morning with my friend James. We stepped up to the first tee; it was a perfectly beautiful east Texas morning. I stepped up and… oops, topped it into the water. Tried again … oops. Okay, one more time… OOPS! I'm thinking we're NOT starting where we left off last time. ONE more time, "Come on, Hood, find your swing," finally, decent contact. Thankfully, I doubled that hole (ok, I didn't count those first three shots, sue me), but I finished with some dignity. The next hole wasn't pretty either, but I made contact and scored a bogey. On the third hole, bogey again. Then on the fourth hole, I FOUND MY SWING! Par. I finished the front nine ten strokes over par, not good, but if I played decent on the back nine, I could leave with a little bit of my pride in tacked.

The back nine wasn't pretty, but I felt more like myself, had more confidence in my game, and had more "faith" in my clubs. Also, being with my friend James helped. We have a very competitive friendship, especially when it comes to golf. He didn't have his best game, either. He finished the front nine two strokes ahead of me. Even though it was unspoken, I could hear those words in my head, "Oh, it's on!" We were friendly and supportive of each other, but on the inside, you know, we were both competing to outdo the other. We finished the back nine tied, which meant he won by two strokes. I was happy for my friend.

What I haven't told you about my friend and the circumstance around the game is that two days before, his wife had died. Trisha was a beautiful soul, 46, and they had just celebrated 27 years together in marriage. He was devastated. I took a chance to ask him to give me 4 hours of his time; I thought it might help him get away from all the noise and focus on his grief. I wasn't sure he would be able to do it or even want to, but he agreed. In the beginning, it was heartbreaking; we both cried and talked about Trisha; the last time they golfed together, what he loved about her, and the memories he will hold onto all the time we were golfing. It was during the beginning of our run when it clicked with me, "You know, buddy, what we're trying to do in our golf game, you need to do in your life, 'find your swing.'" I can't imagine what he was/is going through, and there is nothing that can take away the pain and grief of his loss, but I told him, "This is something you will never get over; you can only try and get through it."

Through the round, we continued to talk and play; our competitive juices began flowing, and, in the midst of our crying and grief, we started to play golf. Now my boy can drive the ball, and when that kicked in, I could feel his confidence and pride take hold. I am so proud of his courage and strength.

If we play this game of life long enough, there will come a time when we face the greatest challenge of our life. It will break us to our very core and consume every thought and feeling. Feelings of loss and hopelessness, like someone has pulled the plug out of your soul and everything you are has drained out of you, but we still have to get up the next day and play the game. Where to begin? How to begin? How to find the feelings to even want to begin? At the very least, compete, step up to the ball, take your club and give it your best shot. I love my friend and will do my best to be there for him through his journey, but I told him, "James, don't lose you; I need you, your family and friends need you, and this world needs you… I need you to be you; find your swing," in the midst of all that is going on inside of you, play the game.

THE LAST HOLE

There will be a day when I play my last round of golf. The last time I drive, hit, pitch, putt, and putt again (that's kind of how my game goes) on the 18th hole. Since I don't know when that day will happen, I play each round as if it's my last.

I don't want to get to the end of my last round and realize I was grumpy all the way through it. One of my favorite moments every time I play is standing on the last tee box, taking a deep breath, and reflecting on the day. I take in the beauty around me and reflect on the moments that touched and inspired me, the disappointments that made me rise up and overcome, and the people I shared this time with for a little while.

When it's all over, and we've putted out and shaken hands for the last time, there's always a mixture of sadness, contentment, and gratefulness.

I'm sad that this time, this moment, is over. It now joins so many other great memories of special times on the course, some more memorable than others, but all of them are a part of my journey. We've been able to play some amazing venues, beautiful courses, and memorable holes.

I'm content with the knowledge and understanding that every round revealed something about me and my game. If I'm honest, I'm not that content with my score or how I played. I am content with my effort. The most obvious is my need and desire to play better. Every round says something about my game. Even if this round was my last, I'm content that I gave it my best effort.

I'm grateful that I was able to play from my heart, my passion, and my love for the game. Golf is a great reminder of how I want to live my everyday life.

THE 19TH HOLE

I did a little research and came across this tidbit about the history of the 19th hole.

From The Evening Telegraph (Dundee, Angus, Scotland) of Friday 5th December 1890:

GOLF:

"The Monifieth Club finish their golfing season tomorrow, when they play for medals, and a number of clubs, balls, and other prizes. With such inducements, there ought to be a big turnout, but the shortness of the day will prevent many from getting around who would otherwise be on the green. They are to hold their annual supper shortly, when some of the members will be sure to exhibit as much, if not more, enthusiasm and heartiness at the 'nineteenth' hole as they do on the green on cup and medal days. "

It doesn't matter whether you're a beginner or an old pro, "The 19th Hole" is the best part of playing the game. Gathering with friends, old and new, for a time of refreshment and storytelling. The more serious golfer is tallying up the scores and settling side bets. It's a special place full of life, energy, and friendship.

"The 19th Hole" is a reminder of what makes life great; going out competing with the elements, overcoming the obstacles faced on the course, facing off with friend and foe, and when it's all said and done, reflect and look forward to the next opportunity with friends.

Whether you're an avid golfer or not, I hope you were able to see some of life's truths in what has been shared. For me, one of the biggest lessons is As long as you are able, play the game. I'm 60 as of this writing, which means I've been chasing that little ball for 46 years. My game is average at best, and my body hurts, but I still find a way to get on the course, be with my friends and do the best I can.

If you take nothing else from what I've shared, realize that **the golf ball doesn't lie**, but neither does the heart and spirit. Go ahead, see how far you can hit it!

AUTHOR BIOGRAPHY

Larry and Linda Hood

live in Odessa, Texas. Golfing is an important part of their relationship, their favorite places to golf are: Horseshoe Bay,Tx. Myrtle Beach, S. C. Ruidoso, N. M. de Cordova Bend, Tx. and their home Course at Ratliff Ranch in Odessa, Tx.

They have two grown children and their spouses who share their love of Golf; Hayley & Stetson (grandson - Hudson), Patrick & Haylie D. (Grandsons - Mason, Ben & Brooks)

Larry has a bachelors in Business Administration and a Masters in Divinity. He has spent his adult life ministering to youth and adults. The focus of his ministry is discipleship, leadership and life-skills. He has lead and spoken at retreats, conferences, men's groups, and congregations.

If you would like to contact him for a speaking engagement, his email is: _L3Lhood@yahoo. com_